Clouds

by Jenny Fretland VanVoorst

Bullfrog Books

Ideas for Parents and Teachers

Bullfrog Books let children practice reading informational text at the earliest reading levels. Repetition, familiar words, and photo labels support early readers.

Before Reading

- Discuss the cover photo. What does it tell them?

- Look at the picture glossary together. Read and discuss the words.

Read the Book

- "Walk" through the book and look at the photos. Let the child ask questions. Point out the photo labels.

- Read the book to the child, or have him or her read independently.

After Reading

- Prompt the child to think more. Ask: Can you spot the differences in the shapes of clouds? What kind of weather comes with differently shaped clouds?

Bullfrog Books are published by Jump!
5357 Penn Avenue South
Minneapolis, MN 55419
www.jumplibrary.com

Library of Congress Cataloging-in-Publication Data

Names: Fretland VanVoorst, Jenny, 1972– author.
Title: Clouds / by Jenny Fretland VanVoorst.
Description: Minneapolis, MN: Jump!, Inc., [2016] 2017 | Series: Weather watch | "Bullfrog Books are published by Jump!" | Audience: Ages 5–8. Audience: K to grade 3. | Includes bibliographical references and index.
Identifiers: LCCN 2016013598 (print)
LCCN 2016014178 (ebook)
ISBN 9781620313879 (hardcover: alk. paper)
ISBN 9781624964343 (ebook)
Subjects: LCSH: Clouds—Juvenile literature.
Classification: LCC QC921.35 .F74 2016 (print)
LCC QC921.35 (ebook) | DDC 551.57/6—dc23
LC record available at http://lccn.loc.gov/2016013598

Editor: Kirsten Chang
Series Designer: Ellen Huber
Book Designer: Molly Ballanger
Photo Researcher: Olympia Shannon

Photo Credits: All photos by Shutterstock except: Alamy, 16, 17; iStock, 14–15, 18, 23br; Thinkstock, 4, 8–9, 20–21, 22br.

Printed in the United States of America at Corporate Graphics in North Mankato, Minnesota.

Table of Contents

Look Up!

Look up.

What do you see?

Clouds!

Clouds are made
of water vapor.

Some are fat
and puffy.

Some are thin
and stringy.

Clouds tell us
the weather.

Will it rain?

Will it snow?

Look up!

Some clouds are puffy.

They look like cotton balls.

What do they mean?

The weather
will be dry.

Lia does not
need her boots.

Big, dark clouds are
full of moisture.

Heavy droplets
fall to the ground.

droplets

13

It's raining!
Ben grabs
an umbrella.

Today is very cold.
Look up! The clouds
are low and heavy.

Snow may fall later.
Meg grabs her coat.

17

Look! The clouds are piled up.

That means a storm is coming.

Jeb plays inside today.

What will the weather be like where you are?

Look up!

Types of Clouds

cirrus
These thin, stringy clouds are a sign that the weather is likely to change soon.

cumulonimbus
These clouds are often called thunderheads. They are a sign that a storm is on the way.

cumulus
These puffy, white clouds are a sign of nice weather.

stratus
Rain often falls from these low, flat clouds.

Picture Glossary

droplets
Very small drops.

stringy
Stretched out to
look like string.

moisture
Wetness.

vapor
Fine particles
of a liquid, such
as water, that
are suspended
in the air.

Index

To Learn More

Learning more is as easy as 1, 2, 3.

1) Go to www.factsurfer.com

2) Enter "clouds" into the search box.

3) Click the "Surf" button to see a list of websites.

With factsurfer.com, finding more information is just a click away.

24